growing
together
in Christ

homebuilders
COUPLES SERIES®

growing together in Christ

by
david
sunde

Little Rock, Arkansas

GROWING TOGETHER IN CHRIST
FamilyLife Publishing®
5800 Ranch Drive
Little Rock, Arkansas 72223
1-800-FL-TODAY • FamilyLife.com

FLTI, d/b/a FamilyLife®, is a ministry of Campus Crusade for Christ International®

ISBN: 978-1-60200-331-6

Design: Brand Navigation, LLC

Cover image: iStockphoto.com/AVAVA/Artemis Gordon

Printed in the United States of America

15 14 13 12 11   3 4 5 6 7

FAMILYLIFE®

Unless the LORD builds the house,
those who build it labor in vain.

PSALM 127:1

The HomeBuilders Couples Series®

Building Your Marriage to Last
Improving Communication in Your Marriage
Resolving Conflict in Your Marriage
Mastering Money in Your Marriage
Building Teamwork in Your Marriage
Growing Together in Christ
Building Up Your Spouse
Managing Pressure in Your Marriage

The HomeBuilders Parenting Series®

Improving Your Parenting
Establishing Effective Discipline for Your Children
Guiding Your Teenagers
Raising Children of Faith

welcome to homebuilders

Marriage should be enjoyed, not endured. It is meant to be a vibrant relationship between two people who love each other with passion, commitment, understanding, and grace. So secure is the bond God desires between a husband and a wife that he uses it to illustrate the magnitude of Christ's love for the church (Ephesians 5:25–33).

Do you have that kind of love in your marriage?

Relationships often fade over time as people drift apart—but only if the relationship is left unattended. We have a choice in the matter; our marriages don't have to grow dull. Perhaps we just need to give them some attention.

That's the purpose behind the HomeBuilders Couples Series— to provide you a way to give your marriage the attention it needs and deserves. This is a biblically based small-group study because, in the Bible, God has given the blueprint for building a loving and secure marriage. His plan is designed to enable a man and a woman to grow together in a mutually satisfying relationship and then to reach out to others with the love of Christ. Ignoring God's plan may lead to isolation and, in far too many cases, the breakup of the home.

Whether your marriage needs a complete makeover or just a few small adjustments, we encourage you to consult God's design. Although written nearly two thousand years ago, Scripture still speaks clearly and powerfully about the conflicts and challenges men and women face.

Do we really need to be part of a group? Couldn't we just go through this study as a couple?

While you could work through the study as a couple, you would miss the opportunity to connect with friends and to learn from one another's experiences. You will find that the questions in each session not only help you grow closer to your spouse, but they also create an environment of warmth and fellowship with other couples as you study together.

What does it take to lead a HomeBuilders group?

Leading a group is much easier than you may think, because the leader is simply a facilitator who guides the participants through the discussion questions. You are not teaching the material but are helping the couples discover and apply biblical truths. The special dynamic of a HomeBuilders group is that couples teach themselves.

The study guide you're holding has all the information and guidance you need to participate in or lead a HomeBuilders group. You'll find leader's notes in the back of the guide, and additional helps are posted online at FamilyLife.com/Resources.

What is the typical schedule?

Most studies in the HomeBuilders Couples Series are six to eight weeks long, indicated by the number of sessions in the guide. The sessions are designed to take sixty minutes in the group with a project for the couples to complete between sessions.

Isn't it risky to talk about your marriage in a group?

The group setting should be enjoyable and informative—and non-threatening. **THREE SIMPLE GROUND RULES** will help ensure that everyone feels comfortable and gets the most out of the experience:

1. Share nothing that will embarrass your spouse.
2. You may pass on any question you do not want to answer.
3. If possible, as a couple complete the HomeBuilders project between group sessions.

What other help does FamilyLife offer?

Our list of marriage and family resources continues to grow. Visit FamilyLife.com to learn more about our:

- Weekend to Remember® getaway, The Art of Marriage™ and other events;
- slate of radio broadcasts, including the nationally syndicated *FamilyLife Today*®, *Real FamilyLife with Dennis Rainey*®, and *FamilyLife This Week*®;
- multimedia resources for small groups, churches, and community networking;
- interactive products for parents, couples, small-group leaders, and one-to-one mentors; and
- assortment of blogs, forums, and other online connections.

about the author

David Sunde serves internationally with Global Community Resources of Campus Crusade for Christ. He and his wife, Sande, have authored several resources for Christians in the marketplace. They are the parents of three children and grandparents of thirteen. David and Sande live in Colorado.

contents

One of the most flawed assumptions we could make is that spiritual growth will just happen. Far too many Christians become stale and stagnant because they assume that growth will occur just because they are involved in religious activities. But the New Testament teaches that spiritual growth is the result of some basic and fundamental steps that each of us is responsible to take.

This study will demonstrate that spiritual growth best occurs as we are accountable to each other. Marriage presents us with the best of opportunities as one spouse helps the other in the pursuit of spiritual maturity. There is no greater intimacy, no higher joy for a married couple than growing together in Christ.

Through this study, you will be challenged to grow deeper in Christ. May you enjoy the adventure. Together.

—Dennis & Barbara Rainey

1 Essentials for Establishing Growth as a Couple

The Christian life is one of exciting growth as you establish a solid relationship with Christ.

warm-up

Meaningful Moments

Introduce yourselves as a couple by telling the group one of the following things about your relationship.

- A particularly fun getaway or vacation you've had as a couple and what made it special
- The most meaningful spiritual experience you've had as a couple

Whether it is the rapid development of a newborn child or the blossoming of a fruit tree, all living things are meant to grow. Our life in Christ, too, should be an exciting experience of growth.

Case Study: Slow Growing

Ryan's credentials were impeccable: He had received top grades in high school, had graduated with honors from Harvard, and had breezed through Harvard Medical School. He had successfully endured the grueling life of an intern and completed a residency in pediatric surgery. After he began his private practice, it blossomed. Ryan was confident, skilled, and well liked.

When Ryan and his wife, Melissa, joined a local church, their pastor quickly tapped them for teaching and leadership roles. That's when the troubles started.

Melissa enthusiastically began teaching a Sunday school class for third graders, and it did very well. But soon after Ryan began teaching a class for young couples, class attendance began to fall.

"His teaching is weak," one couple said. "He hardly knows the Bible."

When the pastor asked Ryan how often he studied the Bible, Ryan replied, "Melissa seems to enjoy that more than I do. Besides, she has the freedom to attend weekly Bible studies. I never have the time."

Ryan was also chairing a committee to look at options for building a new sanctuary. Soon the pastor began hearing reports of contention in the meetings. "Ryan wants to run things his own way," one man said. "He blows up when anyone questions him."

While Ryan's pediatric clinic flourished, he seemed out of his element at church. "You'd never know that he's been a Christian for twenty years," sighed his pastor.

1. Do you agree that Ryan seems immature for a twenty-year Christian? What makes him seem immature?

2. Read 1 Corinthians 3:1–3. What does it mean to be a spiritual infant?

3. What do you think Christians need to do to mature in their faith?

4. Read John 15:1–5. According to this passage, what is the key to spiritual growth? What does it mean to abide in Christ?

5. Read 2 Corinthians 5:17. In what ways do people become new creations when they become Christians? How do their lives change?

homebuilders principle: The true Christian life is an exciting, everyday relationship with the living Christ.

Obstacles to Growth

6. What prevents some Christians from growing spiritually?

7. Have you ever gone through a period in your life when you didn't seem to grow in your faith? If possible, tell what characterized your life at that time. Why do you think you weren't growing?

Growing Together

8. You play a key role in your spouse's spiritual growth. What are some ways you can encourage your spouse in this area?

9. If both you and your spouse continue to grow together in your relationships with Christ, how will this affect your marriage?

homebuilders principle: As you each grow closer to God, you will experience greater oneness in your marriage.

make a date

Set a time for you and your spouse to complete the HomeBuilders project together before the next group meeting. You will be asked at the next session to share an insight or experience from the project.

date _____ time _____

location _____

On Your Own

Answer the following questions:

1. Draw a graph that traces your spiritual growth pattern since you became a Christian. Have your line go up during times of spiritual growth, be flat during times of spiritual stagnation, and go down during times of falling away from God.

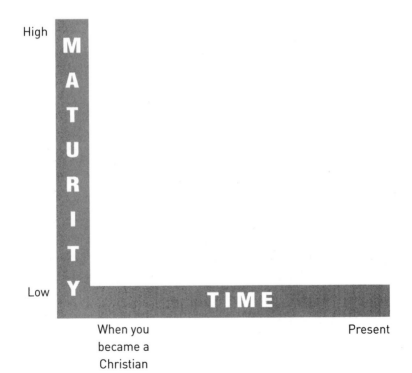

High

Low

M
A
T
U
R
I
T
Y

TIME

When you
became a
Christian

Present

2. What factors influenced the various phases in your spiritual growth?

3. What are three things your spouse can do to help you grow spiritually?

4. What spiritual growth have you seen in your spouse's life since you've known him or her?

5. In what areas do you hope to grow most in the next year?

With Your Spouse

1. Take a look at the spiritual growth charts you filled out, and explain your reasoning to each other.

2. Differing rates of Christian growth sometimes cause conflict between spouses. To what extent have you experienced this in your marriage? What can you do to promote growing at similar rates in the future?

3. Share your responses to the questions you answered on your own.

4. Conclude your time by listing what you commit to do during this course to make your spiritual growth together a priority. You might want to include items such as keeping "dates," working through HomeBuilders projects, participating in the study group, and encouraging each other.

5. Pray together, asking God to guide you to new levels of spiritual growth in your marriage.

Remember to take your calendar to the next session for Make a Date.

2

The Power of
Prayer in Marriage

Prayer promotes growth in your relationships with God and with your spouse.

warm-up

Practiced Prayer

Whether or not you grew up in a Christian home, you learned about prayer as you observed the attitudes and practices of family, friends, church members, or even characters in television shows and movies.

1. For fun, recite aloud any memorized prayers you still remember.

2. As a child, what was your concept of prayer?

3. How has your concept of prayer changed since you were a child?

Project Report

If you completed the HomeBuilders project from the first session, share one thing you learned.

Barriers and Benefits

1. Why do you think many Christian couples spend little time together in prayer?

2. What do these passages from God's Word say about how prayer can help you grow in your relationship with God?

   • 2 Chronicles 7:14

   • Matthew 6:6

- Matthew 26:41

- Philippians 4:6–7

- James 1:5

- James 5:16

3. If you've ever experienced one of the truths of the previous verses, tell what happened. How have you received God's wisdom or peace, or how have you experienced God's presence through prayer?

Basic Components of Prayer

Because prayer is talking with God, it's a wonderful way to develop your relationship with him. But many people don't know how to pray.

The psalms are among the best known and best loved writings of all literature. Many psalms are actually prayers, and from them we can learn about the basic components of prayer.

Praise

The element of prayer that the psalms are best known for is praise. Throughout the psalms David and other writers express their adoration of God.

4. Read Psalm 96:1–10. What does it mean to praise God? If a person were to consistently spend time praising God, how would that affect the way that person looks at problems he or she faces?

5. What could you praise God for right now? Tell the group about it.

Confession

In Psalm 51, one of the greatest examples of confession in the Bible, David confesses his sins of committing adultery with Bathsheba and sending her husband off to be killed in battle.

6. Read Psalm 51:1–13. What was David seeking in this confession? What was the attitude behind his confession?

7. Read 1 John 1:9. What does God promise to do when we confess sin? Why is confession important in our relationship with God?

Supplication

Psalm 34 is often read and quoted to encourage people to bring their needs and desires to God in prayer.

8. Read Psalm 34:4–18. Reflect on the effect that prayer can have in a person's life. Share your thoughts with your group.

Praying Together

9. Read Matthew 18:19–20. How do these verses relate to praying together as a couple? How would your marriage benefit if you were to pray together more consistently?

homebuilders principle: Praying together affirms your unified dependence on God and helps produce the cleansing, humility, and unity essential to spiritual growth in marriage.

make a date

Set a time for you and your spouse to complete the HomeBuilders project together before the next group meeting. You will be asked at the next session to share an insight or experience from the project.

date _____ time _____

location _____

On Your Own

Answer the following questions:

1. What insight did you gain about prayer in marriage from this session?

2. How well do you feel you and your spouse do at praying together? What is one thing you could do to improve in this area?

3. When you pray, on which of the three components (praise, confession, and supplication) do you spend the most time? On which do you spend the least ?

4. Using Psalm 96 as a guide, spend time praising God for who he is and what he has done in your life. You may want to write a list of specific things to praise God for.

5. Read 1 John 1:9. Spend a few moments confessing any sins that are blocking growth in your relationship with God. Then thank God for forgiving those sins.

6. What needs do you have or know about? List them as prayer requests, then pray through the list. NOTE: Use the pages labeled "Prayer Journal" at the back of this book.

With Your Spouse

1. Share with each other one of the following:

   - the most humorous thing you remember praying for as a child
   - the cutest or most humorous thing you've heard about a child praying for

2. Share your responses to the questions you answered on your own.

3. What do you see as the value of praying together?

4. Choose a time and place for regular prayer together.

5. One tool that can help make prayer meaningful and significant in your life is a prayer journal. In it you enter particular concerns and the date. Leave some space between entries so that later you can record what happened after your prayers.

As part of this study, keep a prayer journal for the next few weeks. Doing this will give you a measurable way of seeing God at work in your lives. Few experiences are more exciting!

6. Now it's time to practice what you've been learning. Talk about one need in your lives right now—it could be something you'd like to see God accomplish at work, in your children, in your marriage, or in any other part of your life. Take turns praying simple one- or two-sentence prayers. Spend a few minutes praising God, confessing sins as you need to, and telling God about your needs and the needs of others.

Remember to take your calendar to the next session for Make a Date.

3

The Guidebook
for Growth

The greatest book ever written is God's gift to help you grow closer to him and to your spouse.

warm-up

I Love to Tell the Story

Begin by sharing one of the following with the group:

- a favorite Bible story from your childhood and why it's a favorite
- a Bible passage that has been particularly meaningful in your life or in your marriage
- your thoughts about the Bible's relevance to your life

Project Report

Share one thing you learned from the HomeBuilders project from last session.

The Book of Books

A brief essay by Henry Van Dyke expresses how the Bible is a timeless treasure.

Born in the East and clothed in Oriental form and imagery, the Bible walks the ways of all the world with familiar feet, and enters land after land to find its own everywhere. It has learned to speak in hundreds of languages to the heart of man. It comes into the palace to tell the monarch that he is a servant of the Most High, and into the cottage to assure the peasant that he is a son of God. Children listen to its stories with wonder and delight, and wise men ponder them as parables of life. It has a word of peace for the time of peril, a word of comfort for the time of calamity, a word of light for the hour of darkness. Its oracles are repeated in the assembly of the people, and its counsels whispered in the ear of the lonely. The wicked and the proud tremble at its warnings, but to the wounded and the penitent it has a mother's voice. The wilderness and the solitary place have been made glad by it, and the fire on the hearth has lit the reading of its well-worn pages. It has woven itself into our dearest dreams; so that love, friendship, sympathy and devotion, memory and hope put on the beautiful garments of its treasured speech, breathing of frankincense and myrrh.

1. What thoughts about the Bible does this essay inspire in you? What benefits have you gained from reading and studying the Bible?

2. Read Psalm 119:160. Why is it so important in today's culture to know that God's Word presents absolute, everlasting truth?

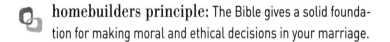 **homebuilders principle:** The Bible gives a solid foundation for making moral and ethical decisions in your marriage.

Our Personal Treasure

3. Read Psalm 19:7–11. How can God's Word revive the soul?

4. Read Psalm 119:49–50. How does the Bible comfort you in difficult times?

5. What obstacles keep you from studying the Bible consistently as an individual? As a couple?

homebuilders principle: If you value knowing the Bible and applying it to your life, you will discover the spiritual food your souls need to survive.

Step-by-Step Study

6. If you have studied the Bible together as a couple, how have you done it? What has worked for you?

7. If you were to study the Bible with your spouse on a regular basis, what effect do you think this would have on your relationship?

8. Using the three-step approach outlined below, do a brief study of Philippians 4:6–7. Read the passage twice, slowly and carefully. Then, as a couple, proceed through the three steps. After a few minutes share some of your observations with the group.

A THREE-STEP APPROACH TO BIBLE STUDY

Step One: What does it say? Observe the text and the relationships of the words in the passage you are studying. Seek to understand what the passage is saying.

Step Two: What does it mean? Dig into the passage. Ask questions such as "Why did the author say this? What message was the author trying to get across?"

Step Three: What does it mean to me? Apply to your life what you have learned. Determine what difference this truth can and will make in your life right now.

Step One: What does it say?

- What is the main idea of this passage?

Step Two: What does it mean?

- What does it mean to "not be anxious about anything"?

- How does the peace of God surpass "all understanding"?

Step Three: What does it mean to me?

- Have you ever experienced God's peace after you prayed about a situation that had been making you anxious? Tell about the experience if you can.

- What are some situations that you're anxious about right now? What does this passage say you should do about your anxiety? Right now spend a few minutes in prayer about these situations, and ask for God's guidance and peace.

homebuilders principle: Growing together in Christ as a couple requires regular study of God's Word.

make a date

Set a time for you and your spouse to complete the HomeBuilders project together before the next group meeting. You will be asked at the next session to share an insight or experience from the project.

date _____ time _____

location _____

On Your Own

Answer the following questions:

1. What is one insight or discovery you gained from this session?

2. When has the Bible made a significant difference in your life?

3. How would studying the Bible regularly help you, as an individual and as a couple?

4. What needs could the Bible help you with right now?

5. What is currently preventing you from spending time in God's Word individually and as a couple?

With Your Spouse

1. Share the following with each other:

   - the book (other than the Bible) that has had the greatest influence on your life and why,
   - the person who has had the greatest influence on your life and why,
   - the influence the Bible has had on your life and why.

2. Share your responses to the questions you answered on your own. Listen nonjudgmentally, being sensitive to ways you and your spouse can help each other spend meaningful time in the Word individually and together.

3. Rough out a plan for reading and studying the Bible together regularly. There are numerous approaches to studying the Bible; here are just a few to get you started:

Reading Programs

   - Read through the Bible in a year. Several programs are available to help you do that.

- Read a chapter of the Gospel according to John each day. It's probably the best single presentation of the gospel in the Bible.
- Choose a Bible book to read, and each day read in it until you find something that really hits you.

Study Programs

- Explore different books of the Bible. Pick a book, preferably a short one to start with, and read through it two or three times, noting themes and favorite verses. Use the three-step plan described in the Blueprints section.
- Examine the lives and experiences of people in the Bible. Choose a character—Joseph, Daniel, Esther, Peter, or any character you relate to—and find all the passages in which this character is mentioned. Look for clues to the person's strengths, weaknesses, and motivations. Seek to apply what you learned from this person's experiences.
- Study key words in the Bible. Choose a word such as peace or humility, and using a Bible concordance, look up verses in which the word appears.

4. Decide on a schedule for studying the Bible together as a couple.

5. Pray together for current needs and concerns, and commit your plans and purposes to the Lord. Ask God to help you succeed in studying the Bible together as you seek to grow together in Christ.

Remember to take your calendar to the next session for Make a Date.

4 Growing Together Through the Holy Spirit

When you draw upon the Holy Spirit's power, you will experience growth in your life and in your marriage relationship.

warm-up

Case Study: Power Shortage

When Jacob and Corey became Christians two years ago, their lives changed dramatically. They began to study the Bible regularly, getting up early every morning to make sure they could read God's Word and pray together before their busy day began.

Jacob and Corey go to church every Sunday morning. Corey sings in the choir, and they attend a small group together. Jacob has even gone on overnight camping trips with the junior high group a couple of times.

Though Jacob and Corey appear to be model young believers, lately they have confessed to frustration in their spiritual lives. The joy is fading. They feel so apprehensive about telling their friends and neighbors about Jesus that they just don't say anything. And then they feel guilty.

At times they seem to be just going through the motions with all these Christian activities, and the Christian life is becoming boring. For all their efforts, they don't really feel close to God, and they don't feel his presence and power.

1. What may be wrong in Jacob's and Corey's relationships with God?

Project Report

Share one thing you learned from the HomeBuilders project from last session.

The Holy Spirit in Us

2. If someone were to ask you, "What is the Holy Spirit?" how would you answer?

3 Why do you think many Christians seem confused or uncertain
   about the ministry of the Holy Spirit?

4. Read Ephesians 3:14–19. What will you be missing if you try
   to live the Christian life in your own strength?

5. What do the following passages say about your relationship
   with the Holy Spirit?

   • John 14:16–17

   • John 16:13–15

PICTURE THIS

Line up side by side, with each person holding an uninflated balloon and facing in the same direction. When your leader gives the signal, throw your balloon as far out in front of you as you can.

Retrieve your balloon and inflate it. Don't tie it off, but hold the opening closed so the air doesn't escape. Again line up with the other group members, aim your balloon out in front of you, and at your leader's signal let it go. After the confusion and laughter, discuss the following questions:

- Which time did the balloon travel a greater overall distance?
- Which time did the balloon end up somewhere unexpected?
- What made the difference in the way the balloon traveled?
- Which time was more fun?
- How could this illustrate the Holy Spirit's power to work in and through our lives?

- Acts 1:8

- Romans 8:26–27

- 2 Timothy 1:14

homebuilders principle: The Holy Spirit provides the power you need to live for God on a daily basis.

Living by the Holy Spirit

6. Read Galatians 5:16–23. What impact do the "desires of the flesh" have on a marriage? What about the "fruit of the Spirit"?

7. What do you think it means to "walk by the Spirit"? How can you do that in your marriage?

8. Read 1 John 1:5–10. What must we do before the Holy Spirit will work in us?

9. Read 1 John 5:14–15. What will God do if you ask him to take control of your life through the Holy Spirit?

10. Read Romans 15:13. What difference will it make to you and your spouse if you turn your life over to God's control? If you can, describe how the Holy Spirit has made a difference in your life and in your marriage.

If you would like the power of the Holy Spirit in your life and your marriage, give God control of your life. Confess your sins, and let the Holy Spirit take over. To live consistently in the power of the Holy Spirit, you need to make certain that you are living under God's control daily. Silently offer the following prayer if it reflects the desire of your heart:

> *Dear God, I need you. I acknowledge that I have been in control of my life and that I have sinned against you. I*

ask for your forgiveness and thank you that you have forgiven my sins through Christ's death on the cross for me. I now ask you to take control of my life again. Empower and guide me through your Holy Spirit. As an expression of my faith, I now thank you for guiding my life through the Holy Spirit. I pray this in Jesus' name. Amen.

For more information about how to live by the Holy Spirit, be sure to read "Our Problems, God's Answers," beginning on page 63.

homebuilders principle: The presence and power of the Holy Spirit will help you grow spiritually and will enrich your marriage relationship.

make a date

Set a time for you and your spouse to complete the HomeBuilders project together before the next group meeting. You will be asked at the next session to share an insight or experience from the project.

date _____ time _____

location _____

On Your Own

Answer the following questions:

1. From this session, explain one insight you gained about the role of the Holy Spirit in your marriage.

2. How would your marriage be different if both you and your spouse truly lived by the Holy Spirit?

3. In what areas of your life do you most need God's guidance and power?

4. Take a few minutes to look again at Galatians 5:16–23. As you look back at your life during the last few months, would you say you've been living mostly by the desires of the flesh or by the Spirit? How would you characterize your resulting lifestyle?

5. What is one practical way your spouse can encourage you to "walk by the Spirit"?

6. It's important to walk in the Spirit on a daily basis. The process of walking in the Spirit is one of continually yielding to God's control in your life. Bill Bright, founder of Campus Crusade for Christ, calls this process "spiritual breathing":

   Exhale: Confess, according to 1 John 1:9, the sin that has broken your stride.

   Inhale: Pray that the Holy Spirit will once again take control of your life, and thank God for the renewal of his powerful presence in your life.

   What is one recent, specific situation in which it would have been good for you to apply this principle?

With Your Spouse

1. Share your responses to the questions you answered on your own.

2. Read Ephesians 5:15–21 together. While you read, think about how these commands can make a difference in your life together. Then brainstorm ways you can incorporate some of these commands into your lives.

3. What actions will you take to assure that both of you daily seek and follow the Holy Spirit's leading?

4. Finish by praying together, committing your plans and purposes to the Lord. Pray that God will help you remain faithful in living daily by the Holy Spirit.

Remember to take your calendar to the next session for Make a Date.

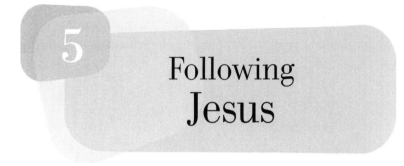

Following
Jesus

Faithfully following Jesus will help you grow together in Christ and in your marriage.

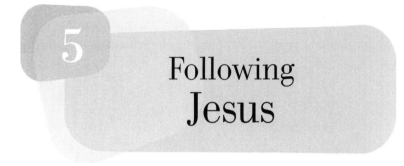

One complaint often raised about Christians is that too many Christians are hypocrites. Do you agree with that? Why or why not?

Complete the following sentence: "A Christian is not a hypocrite when he _____."

Project Report

Share one thing you learned from the HomeBuilders project from last session.

While living on earth, Jesus called men and women to follow him—to become learners or disciples. God still calls men and women to follow him today.

Following Christ

1. Read 2 Corinthians 3:18. What does it mean to be transformed into the image of Christ?

2. Another aspect of following Christ was revealed when Jesus chose his first disciples. Read Matthew 4:18–22, and imagine yourself in this passage.

   • What do you think was difficult about the disciples' decision to follow Christ?

- What did they gain?

3. Name someone you know who seems to have a fervent desire to serve Christ wholeheartedly. What sets that person apart from other people?

4. In what way are you called to follow Christ today?

homebuilders principle: God wants you to follow him wholeheartedly by becoming like Christ and committing your life completely to him.

The Cost and Benefits of Following Christ

5. Read what Christ told his disciples in Matthew 10:37–39. What hits you hardest from this passage?

6. What sacrifices have you made in your life to follow Christ?

7. What do the following verses say about the benefits of following Christ?

- Matthew 11:28–30

- Luke 18:28–30

- John 8:31–32

- John 10:9–10

- Ephesians 3:20–21

8. How would your relationship change if you fully applied Matthew 10:37–39 in your marriage?

homebuilders principle: The benefits of following Christ greatly outweigh the costs.

make a date

Set a time for you and your spouse to complete the HomeBuilders project together before the next group meeting. You will be asked at the next session to share an insight or experience from the project.

date _____ time _____

location _____

homebuilders project

On Your Own

Answer the following questions:

1. From this session, describe the insight about following Jesus that has had the most impact on you.

2. Read John 13:34–35. Why do Christians who demonstrate love stand out in today's culture?

3. When have you stood up for Christ or showed love in a way that demonstrated to others how much you love God?

4. Why is it sometimes difficult to follow Jesus in this way?

5. How has God blessed you as you've sought to follow him?

6. What things in your life sometimes keep you from following God? What can you do about these things?

With Your Spouse

1. Share your responses to the questions you answered on your own.

2. Decide on three steps you can take to follow Christ more fully as a couple. List your steps here:

3. Update your prayer journal in the back of the book, noting any answers to prayer or additional requests. Pray through these requests. Also pray that God will grant you success as a couple to follow the steps you listed in the previous question.

4. Read the following prayer silently, and consider whether you can pray it as the honest sharing of your heart with God. If so, pray it aloud together.

Dear God, thank you for drawing me to follow you. With the Holy Spirit as my guide and helper, I seek to follow you in every part of my life. Thank you for forgiving me when I fall short of that goal and for helping me get my focus back on you. Help me to show love to others so the world will see that I am your disciple. Help us draw closer together in our marriage as we draw closer to you. In Jesus' name. Amen.

Remember to take your calendar to the next session for Make a Date.

6

Making
Disciples

If you are growing together as a couple, you will reproduce spiritually and make an impact for God on generations to come.

warm-up

Positive Impact

1. Share how this group has made an impact on your spiritual growth as a couple through the course of this study.

2. Think of someone else who has made an important contribution to your Christian life. How did this person make such an impact?

PICTURE THIS

After the first question in "Positive Impact," use modeling clay to create a representation of something another person has helped develop in your life—a certain character trait or spiritual discipline, for example. Share what you made with the rest of the group. Then divide your clay in half, and make two smaller versions of the same item. Discuss the following questions:

- How was this activity like reproducing yourself as a Christian?
- How was it different?
- From this activity what insights have you gained about making disciples?

Project Report

Share one thing you learned from the HomeBuilders project from last session.

As a result of abiding in Christ, we will bear fruit—we will reproduce ourselves spiritually by helping others become disciples of Jesus.

God Can Use You!

3. Read Matthew 4:18–20. In our last session we looked at this passage to discover what it means to follow Jesus. Now

discuss the following question: What does it mean to become "fishers of men"?

4. Read the following Bible passages, and answer these questions: What types of people does God tend to use to accomplish his purposes on earth? How are these people like and unlike you?

- Exodus 4:10–12

- Isaiah 6:5–8

- Amos 7:14–15

- Matthew 4:18

- Luke 5:27

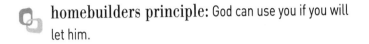 **homebuilders principle:** God can use you if you will let him.

Telling Others

5. Read Matthew 9:36–37. What do you think Jesus meant when he said, "The harvest is plentiful, but the laborers are few"? How true are his words today?

6. Why do you think many Christians are silent about their faith outside the walls of their churches and homes? What can be done about that?

7. Read Matthew 28:19–20. What is your responsibility in making disciples?

The Impact of Disciple Making

8. Share an experience in which God gave you an opportunity to tell someone about your faith. How did that experience affect that person? How did it affect you?

9. Read 2 Timothy 2:2. In what ways have you seen God use you and your spouse together to help others grow in their faith? What other opportunities do you see available to you now?

homebuilders principle: Couples who reproduce spiritually will have a powerful impact on generations to come.

Your Most Important Disciples

10. If you have children, why are they your most important disciples? If you don't have children, whom do you most want

to see growing as a Christian? In either case, what have you done to lead your most important disciples toward a growing faith in Jesus?

11. What is one step you need to take to have a greater spiritual impact on these most important disciples?

make a date

Set a time for you and your spouse to complete the last HomeBuilders project of the study.

date _____ time _____

location _____

homebuilders project

On Your Own

Answer the following questions:

1. From this session, explain the insight about making disciples that has had the most impact on you.

2. How can you get more involved in helping others become followers of Christ?

3. Identify areas in which you need to be better prepared to tell others about Christ:

____ Introducing Christ into a conversation

____ Sharing your faith story

____ Explaining the gospel

____ Guiding a friend to make a faith commitment

____ Other:

4. What can you do to get help in these areas? Write some ideas here.

5. What will you commit to do in reaching out to others to make disciples? Write that commitment here.

6. Personally make your commitment to God in prayer.

With Your Spouse

1. Share with each other what you wrote down and committed to from the individual questions.

2. What might be keeping you as a couple from being used by God to influence others for Christ? What steps should you take to correct this situation?

3. Write down the names of at least four people you would like to see make a faith commitment to Christ or grow in their faith.

4. Discuss the needs you see in the lives of these people and what you have in common that might help you develop relationships with them. What will you do as a couple to reach out to one of the individuals or couples on your list?

5. Together, pray by name for the people you listed. Specifically ask God to use you in sharing Jesus with each person.

6. Now think of your children. What kind of Christians would you like them to be when they become adults?

7. What can you do over the next six months, next year, and next five years to build these qualities into their lives?

8. In what ways would you want your children to be like you when they are grown? In what ways would you want them to be different?

9. Now that this study is over, what steps can you take as an individual and as a couple to continue to grow in Christ?

10. Complete this statement together: "When we die, we want to be remembered as a couple who _____

_____ ."

11. Spend some time in prayer requesting that God will continue working in your relationship to help you grow in Christ together.

where do you go from here?

We hope that you have benefited from this study in the Home-Builders Couples Series and that your marriage will continue to grow as you both submit your lives to Jesus Christ and build according to his blueprints. We also hope that you will reach out to strengthen other marriages in your local church and community. Your influence is needed.

A favorite World War II story illustrates this point clearly.

The year was 1940. The French army had just collapsed under Hitler's onslaught. The Dutch had folded, overwhelmed by the Nazi regime. The Belgians had surrendered. And the British army was trapped on the coast of France in the channel port of Dunkirk.

Two hundred twenty thousand of Britain's finest young men seemed doomed to die, turning the English Channel red with their blood. The Fuehrer's troops, only miles away in the hills of France, didn't realize how close to victory they actually were.

Any attempt at rescue seemed futile in the time remaining. A thin British navy—the professionals—told King George VI that they could save 17,000 troops at best. The House of Commons was warned to prepare for "hard and heavy tidings."

Politicians were paralyzed. The king was powerless. And the Allies could only watch as spectators from a distance. Then as the doom of the British army seemed imminent, a strange fleet appeared on the horizon of the English Channel—the wildest assortment of boats perhaps ever assembled in history. Trawlers, tugs, scows, fishing sloops, lifeboats, pleasure craft, smacks and coasters, sailboats, even the London fire-brigade flotilla. Ships manned by civilian volunteers—English fathers joining in the rescue of Britain's exhausted, bleeding sons.

William Manchester writes in his epic novel *The Last Lion* that what happened in 1940 at Dunkirk seems like a miracle. Not only were most of the British soldiers rescued but 118,000 other Allied troops as well.

Today the Christian home is much like those troops at Dunkirk—pressured, trapped, demoralized, and in need of help. The Christian community may be much like England—waiting for professionals to step in and save the family. But the problem is much too large for them to solve alone.

We need an all-out effort by men and women "sailing" to rescue the exhausted and wounded families. We need an outreach effort by common couples with faith in an uncommon God. For too long, married couples within the church have abdicated to those in full-time vocational ministry the privilege and responsibility of influencing others.

We challenge you to invest your lives in others, to join in the rescue. You and other couples around the world can team together to build thousands of marriages and families and, in doing so, continue to strengthen your own.

Be a HomeBuilder

Here are some practical ways you can make a difference in families today:

- Gather a group of four to seven couples and lead them through this HomeBuilders study. Consider challenging others in your church or community to form additional HomeBuilders groups.
- Commit to continue building marriages by doing another small-group study in the HomeBuilders Couples Series.
- Consider using the *JESUS* film as an outreach. For more information contact FamilyLife at the number or Web site below.
- Host a dinner party. Invite families from your neighborhood to your home, and as a couple share your faith in Christ.
- If you have attended FamilyLife's Weekend to Remember marriage getaway, consider offering to assist your pastor in counseling engaged couples, using the material you received.

For more information about these ministry opportunities, contact your local church or

FamilyLife
PO Box 7111
Little Rock, AR 72223
1-800-FL-TODAY
FamilyLife.com

Every couple has to deal with problems in marriage—communication problems, money problems, difficulties with sexual intimacy, and more. Learning how to handle these issues is important to cultivating a strong and loving relationship.

The Big Problem

One basic problem is at the heart of every other problem in marriage, and it's too big for any person to deal with on his or her own. The problem is separation from God. If you want to experience life and marriage the way they were designed to be, you need a vital relationship with the God who created you.

But sin separates us from God. Some try to deal with sin by working hard to become better people. They may read books on how to control anger, or they may resolve to stop cheating on their taxes, but in their hearts they know—we all know—that the sin problem runs much deeper than bad habits and will take more than our best behavior to overcome it. In reality, we have rebelled against God. We have ignored him and have decided to run our lives in a way that makes sense to us, thinking that our ideas and plans are better than his.

> "For all have sinned and fall short of the glory of God."
> (Romans 3:23)

What does it mean to "fall short of the glory of God"? It means that none of us has trusted and treasured God the way we should. We have sought to satisfy ourselves with other things and have treated them as more valuable than God. We have gone our own way. According to the Bible, we have to pay a penalty for our sin. We cannot simply do things the way we choose and hope it will be okay with God. Following our own plans leads to our destruction.

> "There is a way that seems right to a man, but its end
> is the way to death." (Proverbs 14:12)

> "For the wages of sin is death." (Romans 6:23)

The penalty for sin is that we are separated from God's love. God is holy, and we are sinful. No matter how hard we try, we cannot come up with some plan, like living a good life or even trying to do what the Bible says, and hope that we can avoid the penalty.

God's Solution to Sin

Thankfully, God has a way to solve our dilemma. He became a man through the person of Jesus Christ. Jesus lived a holy life in perfect obedience to God's plan. He also willingly died on a cross to pay our penalty for sin. Then he proved that he is more powerful than sin or death by rising from the dead. He alone has the power to overrule the penalty for our sin.

> "Jesus said to him, 'I am the way, and the truth, and
> the life. No one comes to the Father except through
> me.' " (John 14:6)

"But God shows his love for us in that while we were
still sinners, Christ died for us." (Romans 5:8)

"For the wages of sin is death, but the free gift of
God is eternal life in Christ Jesus our Lord." (Romans
6:23)

The death and resurrection of Jesus have fixed our sin problem.
He has bridged the gap between God and us. He is calling us to come
to him and to give up our flawed plans for running our lives. He
wants us to trust God and his plan.

Accepting God's Solution

If you recognize that you are separated from God, he is calling you
to confess your sins. All of us have made messes of our lives
because we have stubbornly preferred our ideas and plans to his.
As a result, we deserve to be cut off from God's love and his care
for us. But God has promised that if we will acknowledge that we
have rebelled against his plan, he will forgive us and will fix our
sin problem.

"But to all who did receive him, who believed in his
name, he gave the right to become children of God."
(John 1:12)

"For by grace you have been saved through faith. And
this is not your own doing; it is the gift of God, not a
result of works, so that no one may boast." (Ephesians
2:8–9)

When the Bible talks about receiving Christ, it means we acknowledge that we are sinners and that we can't fix the problem ourselves. It means we turn away from our sin. And it means we trust Christ to forgive our sins and to make us the kind of people he wants us to be. It's not enough to intellectually believe that Christ is the Son of God. We must trust in him and his plan for our lives by faith, as an act of the will.

Are things right between you and God, with him and his plan at the center of your life? Or is life spinning out of control as you seek to make your own way?

If you have been trying to make your own way, you can decide today to change. You can turn to Christ and allow him to transform your life. All you need to do is talk to him and tell him what is stirring in your mind and in your heart. If you've never done this, consider taking the steps listed here:

- Do you agree that you need God? Tell God.
- Have you made a mess of your life by following your own plan? Tell God.
- Do you want God to forgive you? Tell God.
- Do you believe that Jesus' death on the cross and his resurrection from the dead gave him the power to fix your sin problem and to grant you the free gift of eternal life? Tell God.
- Are you ready to acknowledge that God's plan for your life is better than any plan you could come up with? Tell God.
- Do you agree that God has the right to be the Lord and Master of your life? Tell God.

"Seek the LORD while he may be found; call upon him while he is near." (Isaiah 55:6)

Here is a suggested prayer:

Lord Jesus, I need you. Thank you for dying on the cross for my sins. I receive you as my Savior and Lord. Thank you for forgiving my sins and giving me eternal life. Make me the kind of person you want me to be.

The Christian Life

For the person who is a follower of Christ—a Christian—the penalty for sin is paid in full. But the effect of sin continues throughout our lives.

> "If we say we have no sin, we deceive ourselves, and the truth is not in us." (1 John 1:8)

> "For I do not do the good I want, but the evil I do not want is what I keep on doing." (Romans 7:19)

The effects of sin carry over into our marriages as well. Even Christians struggle to maintain solid, God-honoring marriages. Most couples eventually realize they can't do it on their own. But with God's help, they can succeed.

To learn more, read the extended version of this article at FamilyLife.com/Resources.

leader's notes

What is the leader's job?

Your role is more of a facilitator than a teacher. A teacher usually does most of the talking and instructing whereas a facilitator encourages people to think and to discover what Scripture says. You should help group members feel comfortable and keep things moving forward.

Is there a structure to the sessions?

Yes, each session is composed of the following categories:

Warm-Up (5–10 minutes): The purpose of Warm-Up is to help people unwind from a busy day and get to know one another better. Typically the Warm-Up starts with an exercise that is fun but also introduces the topic of the session.

Blueprints (45–50 minutes): This is the heart of the study when people answer questions related to the topic of study and look to God's Word for understanding. Some of the questions are to be discussed between spouses and others with the whole group.

HomeBuilders Project (60 minutes): This project is the unique application that couples will work on between the group meetings. Each HomeBuilders project contains two sections: (1) On your own—questions for husbands and wives to answer individually and (2) With your spouse—an opportunity for couples to share their answers with each other and to make application in their lives.

In addition to these regular features, occasional activities are labeled "Picture This." These activities provide a more active or visual way to make a particular point.

What is the best setting and time schedule for this study?

This study is designed as a small-group, home Bible study. However, it can be adapted for more structured settings like a Sunday school class. Here are some suggestions for using this study in various settings:

In a small group

To create a friendly and comfortable atmosphere, we recommend you do this study in a home setting. In many cases the couple that leads the study also serves as host, but sometimes involving another couple as host is a good idea. Choose the option you believe will work best for your group, taking into account factors such as the number of couples participating and the location.

Each session is designed as a sixty-minute study, but we recommend a ninety-minute block of time to allow for more relaxed conversation and refreshments. Be sure to keep in mind one of the cardinal rules of a small group: good groups start *and* end on time. People's time is valuable, and your group will appreciate your respecting this.

In a Sunday school class

If you want to use the study in a class setting, you need to adapt it in two important ways: (1) You should focus on the content of the Blueprints section of each session. That is the heart of the session.

(2) Many Sunday school classes use a teacher format instead of a small-group format. If this study is used in a class setting, the class should adapt to a small-group dynamic. This will involve an interactive, discussion-based format and may also require a class to break into multiple smaller groups.

What is the best size group?

We recommend from four to seven couples (including you and your spouse). If more people are interested than you can accommodate, consider asking someone to lead a second group. If you have a large group, you may find it beneficial to break into smaller subgroups on occasion. This helps you cover the material in a timely fashion and allows for optimum interaction and participation within the group.

What about refreshments?

Many groups choose to serve refreshments, which helps create an environment of fellowship. If you plan to include refreshments, here are a couple of suggestions: (1) For the first session (or two) you should provide the refreshments. Then involve the group by having people sign up to bring them on later dates. (2) Consider starting your group with a short time of informal fellowship and refreshments (15–20 minutes). Then move into the study. If couples are late, they miss only the food and don't disrupt the study. You may also want to have refreshments available again at the end of your meeting to encourage fellowship. But remember to respect the group members' time by ending the session on schedule and allowing anyone who needs to leave to do so gracefully.

What about child care?

Groups handle this differently, depending on their needs. Here are a couple of options you may want to consider:

- Have people be responsible for making their own arrangements.
- As a group, hire someone to provide child care, and have all the children watched in one location.

What about prayer?

An important part of a small group is prayer. However, as the leader, you need to be sensitive to people's comfort level with praying in front of others. Never call on people to pray aloud unless you know they are comfortable doing this. You can take creative approaches, such as modeling prayer, calling for volunteers, and letting people state their prayers in the form of finishing a sentence. A helpful tool in a group is a prayer list. You should lead the prayer time, but allow another couple to create, update, and distribute prayer lists as their ministry to the group.

Find additional help and suggestions for leading your HomeBuilders group at FamilyLife.com/Resources.

The sessions in this study can be easily led without a lot of preparation time. However, accompanying Leader's Notes have been provided to assist you when needed. The categories within the Leader's Notes are as follows:

Objectives

The Objectives focus on the issues that will be presented in each session.

Notes and Tips

This section provides general ideas, helps, and suggestions about the session. You may want to create a checklist of things to include in each session.

Blueprints Commentary

This section contains notes that relate to the Blueprints questions. Not all Blueprints questions will have accompanying commentary notes. The number of the commentary note corresponds to the number of the question it relates to. (For example, the Leader's Notes, session 1, number 5 in the Blueprints Commentary section relates back to session 1, Blueprints, question 5.)

session one

essentials for establishing growth as a couple

Objectives

The Christian life is one of exciting growth as you establish a solid relationship with Christ.

In this session couples will

- discover that a Christian can grow in faith just as a person matures physically,
- examine what prevents some Christians from growing spiritually,
- learn essentials for spiritual growth,
- realize the importance of growing together spiritually as a couple.

Notes and Tips

1. If you have not already done so, you will want to read the information "About Leading a HomeBuilders Group" and "About the Leader's Notes," starting on page 71.

2. As part of the first session, you may want to review with the group some ground rules (see page ix in Welcome to HomeBuilders).

3. At this first meeting collect the names, phone numbers, and e-mail addresses of the group members. You may want to make a list to copy and distribute to the entire group.

4. Because this is the first session, make a special point to tell the group about the importance of the HomeBuilders project. Encourage each couple to make a date for a time to complete the project before the next meeting. Mention that you will ask about this during Warm-Up at the next session.

5. You may want to offer the closing prayer yourself instead of asking others to pray aloud. Many people are uncomfortable praying in front of others, and unless you already know your group well, it may be wise to venture slowly into various methods of prayer. Regardless of how you decide to close, you should serve as a model.

6. If there is room for more people, you may want to remind the group that they can still invite another couple to join them since this study is just under way.

Blueprints Commentary

Here is some additional information about various Blueprints questions. (Note: the numbers below correspond to the Blueprints questions they relate to.) If you share any of these points, do so in a manner that does not stifle discussion by making you the authority with the real answers. Begin your comments by saying things like, "One thing I notice in this passage is . . ." or, "I think another reason for this is . . ."

2. The person described has not grown very much in his or her faith. This person is probably not spending much time reading the Bible and establishing a solid relationship with God. This person acts much the same as a non-Christian.

4. Abiding in Jesus means seeking him, knowing him, and drawing upon his strength. As a branch, you are connected to Christ, and you draw your spiritual lifeblood from him.

6. One reason some Christians haven't grown much may be that they've never had someone close to them challenge them and model the Christian life for them.

9. It's similar to climbing opposite sides of a triangle with God at the top. As you get closer to God, you also get closer to each other.

session two

the power of prayer in marriage

Objectives

Prayer promotes growth in your relationships with God and with your spouse.

In this session couples will

- recall what they learned about prayer as children,
- discover what the Bible says about the benefits of prayer,
- learn three components of prayer,
- understand how consistent prayer can improve their marriage relationship.

Notes and Tips

1. Since this is the second session, your group members have probably warmed up a bit to one another but may not yet feel free to be completely open and honest about their relationships. Don't force the issue. Continue to encourage couples to attend and to complete their projects.

2. You may wish to have extra study guides and Bibles for those who didn't bring theirs.

3. If someone in this session has joined the group for the first time, give a brief summary of the main points of session 1.

Also be sure to introduce those who do not know each other. And consider giving new couples the chance to tell when and where they met.

4. If refreshments are planned for this session, make sure arrangements for them have been made.

5. If your group has decided to use a prayer list, make sure this is covered.

6. If you told the group during the first session that you'd be asking them to share something they learned from the first HomeBuilders project, be sure to ask them. This is an important way for you to establish an environment of accountability.

7. The section on the benefits of prayer is probably the most important section of this session. If your group members can understand that prayer doesn't have to be lifeless—that they can grow spiritually and experience God and his peace—they'll be motivated to pray more.

8. You may want to ask for a volunteer to close the session in prayer. Check ahead of time with people you think might be comfortable praying aloud.

Blueprints Commentary

1. Christian couples often believe they should pray together but just don't do it. They let other activities and priorities take precedence. They may also feel uncomfortable praying together.

2. Here are some ways prayer can help you grow in your relationship with God:

- 2 Chronicles 7:14: When you pray and turn from your wicked ways, you will experience healing and forgiveness.
- Matthew 6:6: When you pray in secret, God will reward you.
- Matthew 26:41: Prayer can keep you from falling into temptation.
- Philippians 4:6–7: Prayer can bring you God's peace.
- James 1:5: Ask for wisdom, and you will receive it.
- James 5:16: Prayer can lead to healing.

4. Praising God means declaring who he is and what he has done for us. Worship and praise raise our awareness of God's presence in our lives. The more we praise God, the more we notice the ways he touches every aspect of our experience. We begin to see our problems more in the context of God's power and control.

6. David wanted to restore his relationship with God. He was totally humble before God.

7. Confession restores our relationship with God after it has been damaged by sin.

8. This psalm not only talks about what God will do to answer our prayers but also what he does in our hearts when we pray.

session three

the guidebook for growth

Objectives

The greatest book ever written is God's gift to help you grow closer to him and to your spouse.

In this session couples will

- consider the value of the Bible as a resource for individuals and couples,
- recall experiences in which the Bible provided specific benefits in their lives,
- practice using observation, interpretation, and application in the study of the Bible.

Notes and Tips

1. Congratulations. With the completion of this session, you will be halfway through this study. It's time for a checkup: How are you feeling? How is the group going? What has worked well so far? What things would you consider changing as you head into the second portion?

2. Session 3 is a unique study in that the Bible is not just the tool but also the topic. Called by some "the least-read best seller of all time," the Bible often is ignored by many of

the people who declare its benefits. As the leader, focus on showing group members that the Bible can actually change their lives. The most significant goal for this session is that people have a positive experience using the Word.

3. Remember the importance of starting and ending on time.

4. As an example to the group, you and your spouse should complete the HomeBuilders project for each session.

5. Greet people as they arrive. Express appreciation for their participation and support in earlier sessions.

6. Note for your next session: you'll need an uninflated balloon for each person.

Blueprints Commentary

2. Today's culture accepts no standards for truth. For many, truth is subjective, depending on the situation, the person, and the need. But we know God's truth is truth for all time.

4. The Word of God helps us see the work of God in history. By remembering how God has worked in the past, we can get a glimpse of how he can work in our lives.

session four

growing together through the Holy Spirit

Objectives

When you draw upon the Holy Spirit's power, you will experience growth in your life and in your marriage relationship.

In this session couples will

- recognize their need for God's help in living the Christian life,
- discuss Bible passages on what the Holy Spirit does within the life of the Christian,
- commit to living by the Holy Spirit.

Notes and Tips

1. The subject of this session is pivotal in the life of all Christians, because the Holy Spirit gives us the ability to live pleasing to God. Without the Spirit, we end up frustrated and defeated as we try to live the Christian life in our own strength. For some in your group, recognizing the work of the Holy Spirit will bring new insight and understanding. Others may know about the Holy Spirit but need help to personally apply that knowledge. Still others may need to recommit to living by the Spirit. Be in prayer before this session that all participants will be receptive to the Holy Spirit's gentle persuasion in their lives.

2. By this time group members should be comfortable with each other. For prayer at the end of this session, you may want to give anyone who wishes an opportunity to pray by asking the group to finish a sentence that starts something like this: "Lord, I want to thank you for _____." Be sensitive to those who are not comfortable doing this.

3. You may want to make some notes right after the meeting to evaluate how things went. Ask yourself questions such as, Did everyone participate? Is there anyone I should follow up with before the next session? Asking yourself questions like these will help you focus.

4. This week you and your spouse may want to write notes of thanks and encouragement to the couples in your group. Thank them for their commitment and contribution, and let them know you are praying for them. (Make a point to pray for them as you write their note.)

Blueprints Commentary

5. If you sense confusion in your group about who the Holy Spirit is, or if any group members are silent and don't know how to answer the question, use that as a springboard for the remainder of the session. Comment that the confusion and silence prove how real the problem is. Even many Christians don't understand who the Holy Spirit is.

   • John 14:16–17: Notice the prepositions used in these two verses: he will be "*with* you forever" (v. 16), and he "will be *in* you" (v. 17). These indicate that our relationship with the Holy Spirit is meant to be an intimate one.

- John 16:13–15: The Holy Spirit is our guide. He helps us understand Scripture, and he discloses the will of God to us.
- Acts 1:8: Notice that Jesus gives the command in the same breath that he mentions the power. He knows we cannot tell others about Christ without the power of the Holy Spirit.
- Romans 8:26–27: The Holy Spirit helps in prayer by interceding for us.
- 2 Timothy 1:14: The Holy Spirit dwells within us.

7. Walking or living by the Spirit means a continual dependence upon the Holy Spirit for wisdom, guidance, and power.

8. The Holy Spirit will work in a heart that is humble toward God. Unconfessed sin can hinder the work of the Holy Spirit in us.

9. God will give us what we ask according to his will. Since we know his will for us is to be controlled by the Spirit, we know he will grant that request.

10. You can experience joy and peace from God.

session five

Objectives

Faithfully following Jesus will help you grow together in Christ and in your marriage.

In this session couples will

- examine the biblical explanation of the responsibilities, costs, and disciplines of discipleship,
- share experiences in which they have sought to live as Jesus' disciples,
- plan specific steps to take as a couple to love and serve others as Jesus' disciples.

Notes and Tips

1. This session and the next are the most challenging of the entire study. These final sessions will encourage your group members to commit their entire lives to following Christ.

2. Those in your group who have come to grips with the work of the Holy Spirit in their lives will welcome the practical help provided in this session. Those who still struggle with surrendering their will to the Spirit will benefit from the insights about the implications of following Jesus. Those

Christians who casually align themselves with some of Jesus' teaching will be seriously challenged.

3. Be sensitive to the varied levels of spirituality among the group. Lovingly nudge them all toward a life of greater commitment. Openly share your own pilgrimage, letting people know how you have struggled in following Jesus and the reasons you continue to be his disciple.

4. As the leader of a small group, you can pray specifically for each person. Why not take time to pray as you prepare for this session?

5. ***Looking ahead:*** If you're going to do the "Picture This" activity in the Warm-Up section of session 6, you'll need some modeling clay for each person.

Blueprints Commentary

1. As Christians, Christ is our example, and we strive to live up to what he teaches us. However, if we are Christians, Christ is also at work in us. (See also Romans 8:9–11 and Galatians 2:20.)

4. Following Jesus is not the same as being simply an armchair observer, as in "I follow the Cubs; I check their place in the standings every week." Following Jesus involves leaving other pursuits and committing ourselves to God's will for our lives no matter what he calls us to do. It means making God the center of our lives.

7. These are some of the benefits of following Christ:

- Matthew 11:28–30: We will find rest for our souls.
- Luke 18:28–30: Whatever we have given up to follow Christ will be given back to us many times over.
- John 8:31–32: The truth of God's Word gives us great personal freedom.
- John 10:9–10: In Christ there is abundant life.
- Ephesians 3:20–21: God will do much more in our lives than we imagine.

session six

making disciples

Objectives

If you are growing together as a couple, you will reproduce spiritually and make an impact for God on generations to come.

In this session couples will

- explore biblical and personal evidence that God can use them to make disciples,
- discuss the need for Christian couples to share their faith through the power of the Holy Spirit,
- consider opportunities for becoming more effective in sharing their faith with others.

Notes and Tips

1. Christians are not meant to be happy, contented people who keep the good news of Jesus Christ to themselves. Making disciples is both an outgrowth of and a catalyst for our growth in Christ. This session focuses on God's supplying the resources we need to reproduce ourselves spiritually. As the leader, you can help your group members learn to depend on the faithful presence of the Holy Spirit in their day-to-day opportunities to share Christ.

2. People are likely to return to previous patterns of living unless they commit to a plan for continuing the progress made during this study. In this final session of the course, encourage couples to take specific steps to keep their marriages growing. For example, you may want to challenge couples to continue having a date night, as they have during this study. Also, you may want the group to consider doing another study from this series.

Blueprints Commentary

3. Encourage people to think about the analogy and how fishing relates to reaching others for Jesus. Here are a few possibilities: We need to go where the "fish" are, that is, where people needing Jesus live, work, and play. We also need to do those things that attract "fish." Fishers of men should look for ways to interest people in the gospel. For example, some non-Christians would be more likely to go with you to hear a well-known Christian football coach talk about his faith than to go with you to church.

5. Many are ready to come to Christ, but more Christians need to be willing to tell them how.

7. God wants all of us to tell others about him. We may have contact with non-Christians who have little contact with any other Christians. You may want to ask group members to think of people in their neighborhoods or at work whom God wants them to tell about Jesus.

8. To get people talking, you might tell about an opportunity you had to explain the gospel to someone. Focus on the indicators that made you feel the gospel should be shared.

   Invite group members to share similar incidents from their experiences. If they find it difficult to think of appropriate situations, tell them to think of times they now recognize as potential opportunities but may have overlooked at the time.

10. If we have children, they will learn not only from our words but from our example. They absorb our attitudes, our mannerisms, our weaknesses, and our strengths, whether we like it or not. And God has given us the responsibility to point them to him as they grow up.

Prayer Journal

Prayer Journal

Prayer Journal

Looking for more ways to help people build their marriages and families?

Thank you for your efforts to help people develop their marriages and families using biblical principles. We recognize the influence that one person—or couple—can have on another, and we'd like to help you multiply your ministry.

FamilyLife is pleased to offer a wide range of resources in various formats. Visit us online at FamilyLife.com, where you will find information about our

- getaways and events, featuring Weekend to Remember, offered in cities throughout the United States,
- multimedia resources for small groups, churches, and community networking,
- interactive products for parents, couples, small-group leaders, and one-to-one mentors, and
- assortment of blogs, forums, and other online connections.